Come Along with Me to the Pasture Now

COME ALONG WITH ME TO THE PASTURE NOW

Arielle Greenberg

Agape Editions
Los Angeles, California   Binghamton, NY

Published by Agape Editions
http://agapeeditions.com
Los Angeles, California & Binghamton, NY

Copyright © 2021 by Arielle Greenberg
All rights reserved

Front Cover:
Photograph by Mark Kelly (Instagram: @mark.kelly.7330763)
Image is used by kind permission of the photographer.

Back Cover:
Author photograph by Daniel Jackson
Photograph by Mark Kelly
Images are used by kind permission of the photographers.

Cover & interior design: Lauren A. Pirosko

Editors: Fox Henry Frazier, Jasmine An, Jessica Walsh
Associate Editor: Enikő Vághy

This book is set in Linux Libertine and Linux Libertine Slanted.

Agape Editions titles are printed using Lightning Source
and distributed by Ingram Content Group.

This title is also available for purchase directly from the publisher.

Library of Congress
Cataloguing-in-Publication Data
Come Along with Me to the Pasture Now // Arielle Greenberg
Library of Congress Control Number 2016935281
Greenberg, Arielle
ISBN 978-1-939675-38-5

9 8 7 6 5 4 3 2 1

FIRST EDITION

for my children, Willa and Jem, and their father, Rob:
I'm so grateful for the many ways you've all come along with me

CONTENTS

Where I Am From	1
The Black Car	5
ORD	6
Woodland Valley Waldorf Fair	11
After a Fever, Before the Date of Confinement, The Year of Our Lord 2009	12
Middle of a Lightning Storm	13
A Little Land	15
I Return to the City	21
Neighbors	23
Lovely Day for a Wedding (and Panic)	24
Other Particular Strangers	26
Lyric I	27
Or, Down the Rabbit Hole	28
Gifts	30
NOTHING IN NATURE IS SAFER THAN NOTHING	31
Note to self:	38
Instead of "Poet of Place"	39
Go back.	41
[today is the last day]	42
I was reading an article	46
"Sitting Around Singing Kumbaya"	47
Three Pear Trees: First Poem of the New Year, 2011	51
Dollars, and The Change	52
Two Fat Braids Crossed at the Crown	55
Flying into the Nation's Capital to Test My Mettle as Some Chattel	57
Poem About Nothing	59
Dear Robyn Gabel, State Representative, 18th District, Illinois,	61
[By the door is a small woven basket on the floor]	63
When You Feel like Crying at a Faculty Meeting	64
A Way Out	66
[am blown]	67
Claim Song Moon, Abundance Moon, Cutting Moon	71
Thunder Hole	73
Counting Breaths	75

Going Up the Country	77
Written One Year Ago Today, in the Same Mood	78
At Forty	81
Acknowledgments	83
About the Author	85

Where I Am From

I am from a big book with five books in it. It is often red: a red book, a red binding. *We were slaves in Egypt; we stood at the bottom of Sinai with a golden calf made of melted bracelets and with tambourines*; etcetera.

My extended blood. Poland, Russia, Lithuania, Romania, Austria, Brooklyn, Queens, Long Island, places I may never go or may never go again but my bones in my face sing these songs anyway, and can be recognized by the more recent immigrants, the natives of each cabbage-souped place.

Of tenements. Of tenements I know nothing but how the word beats in me, beats me. Of how I beat it to death.

I am mixed on the subject, but mostly proud in a useless and illogical manner.

Questions true me. The culture of asking a lilting question, a rocking back-and-forth question. The culture of an angry question full of lilt. The questions in those five red books: *why hast thou forsaken* and *where are* and *why*. Like my daughter, age two, the why-why girl. The how I question the true of all those nations and neighborhoods and tenements, little ghettos all mixed up and rebordered and unvisited. The question of self, of blood, of faith, of God, of books of rules. The rule questions: *why on this night* and *how many stars before* and *if in its mother's milk*.

How untrue it all may be and how history makes it, if not true, then snaked back into its own mouth. My mouth; my family. My mother's milk, that I drank and that I make. The mother I cannot escape, even forty years in a desert, even with a snake close at hand with an apple, even in a language lost and found, in diaspora, in exile, self-imposed or otherwise.

(I wrote all this out in my second and third books. I thought that I was done.)

And so: a new song:

As an adult, I live in New York City from 1993-1998 (pop. 8,245,000) then Syracuse, NY from 1998-2001 (pop. 145,000) then Boston from 2001-2003 (pop. 625,000).

In 2003, I move first to Chicago (pop. 2,700,000) and then to the city north of its border, Evanston (pop. 76,000) for a full-time tenure-track job as an assistant professor, which I hold from 2003-2009.

In other words, from the ages of 21 to 37, I live in cities.

The Black Car

A Higher Power is paving my skull with another layer of concrete again, inches of a hard gray bonnet, a shell over my head. I want to fleck it off in chunks with a putty knife, get to the real head underneath it all, the where I'm from, but it's too deep down and I'm addicted mostly to the pleasurepain of the dull digging knife.

I am following an expensive black car with the vanity plate ABUSED. Is it a boast or a moan, both or neither? A request? I have no theories. The source of the trauma is so deep down.

ORD

Secret trip into the fat helium of O'Hare
        the chiming death-bell rainbow tunnel of Concourse C
        the tinging magic button blues of O'Hare

depart here and land here
        you would be home now
               if you were Chicago
                            & you are Chicago, a bright keyed fog
with a rose on the watertower

On the flat mountain-lack of Chicago
Miriam danced her girls around & tossed their silver bangles into a pyre

who is the buckle on the belt of the bible Midwest
        Illinois word that collapses
                state that falls down
flat into acreage of dark birds and gods big & little too

The you is over in an ocean or icecap, frenetic

Where is the moon and its mama   it is calling to its mama
        behind a building there
               that's scraped the stars off

It is dirty but not dirty as some
It is noisy but maybe noisier than some (less honking)

It has a greater potential for owls

*

Wearing the Chicago coat, something freezy & friezed
in the moon of an Arctic bean, wedding cake'd bridge

forlorn its lining   forlorn blown   flapped
& bones as yet disintegrate

Butcher   Movie of the butcher and knife

Blow-hole to ship's prow   something happening   the Lake

Cite it down
        God-acre
        Forty acre
God it down silver moving skyscrape straightedge blade
    joust the sky of this deep coat

End now where thoust began: in a pocket
with the snowball gone to a holywater spot

    here's a cause (& effect): the babies
Go glue ribbons on the backs of your eyes for them
over Thanksgiving

    Be a peach in this frozen metal cage
Be a Michigan or a cherry with its stone still in
    the burst of grace congealed in a pin-drop
and that is how a baby is borned

Do not end with the wind or grey
    that is the name Chicago

After the stillbirth of my second child in 2007,
I get pregnant again in 2008,
and at the beginning of 2009,
my husband, daughter and I move to Belfast, Maine (pop. 6700)
for my maternity leave, the homebirth of my third child,
and then a one-year sabbatical
during which my husband and I interview
young back-to-the-landers in rural Waldo County.

Woodland Valley Waldorf Fair

Like the bar game—nestle a shaker in its salt, then blow and see if it still stands—I lose my daughter in a storm in a dream. We're at a woodland valley Waldorf fair, all felted contentment, and the next minute she's racing up the stone steps toward the road, and me caught in the crowd with the baby can't get to her quite, and am calling and calling when the thunder claps and all the stone goes slick.

I'm trying to do too much, the salt says. I will lose or slip or topple. Keep the kids close now, the dark cloud says. The hill is steep, the street trafficked at the top, and the climb worse when it's wet.

After a Fever, Before the Date of Confinement, The Year of Our Lord 2009

Afterwards, all the linens we burned or boiled. The sheets
        I stripped into rags and the socks into puppets.

(Sacred in the parlor and profanities in the kitchen.)

Got up to stir the ash and eggshells.

Knelt at my work for it was pain to sit upright,
        criss-cross applesauce or otherwise.

Said to the child, Not your right grand-mother, but even-tempered,
        and she will have you. Will you have her?

This next child I will bear has started its own mind, left mine to scribbling,
        and I take this to indicate the soonness of the birth.

Middle of a Lightning Storm

There seemed to be some kind of friction in the night.

Not fiction.

That's not what I meant.

More like static electricity. Sandpaper. Letters cut from sandpaper to teach you a lesson.

A child behind the door.

A baby placed on his stomach.

Advice needing to be taken but he had to choose the exactly right piece of it. I did.

I had to grade him. I mean guide him.

In the large sanctuary.

It was a quest. A test.

Someone gave a hint: the right piece would come from a woman, a former vice presidential candidate.

We hid in the pew from all the conflicting advice, me and others.

Turns out the right piece of advice was, "Don't commit suicide by walking the dog."

Meant literally.

Meant also as a metaphor.

So I gave the child her bedtime poem.

Gave the baby his milk, turned him on his side.

Spoke to him "as if" human.

Ignored everyone else.

The children put themselves back to sleep.

It was the middle of the night.

Middle of a lightning storm. "All that rain" as per usual.

Lightest night of the year, darkened by weather.

The dog refusing her bed.

The tapping of the rain, the tapping of the roused child, the tapping of the dog's dreaming leg.

A husband who loved me.

The end of a good day, with "end" meant both ways.

It went on and on, like a religion.

A Little Land

1. lately the county has been responding to a call put out by my husband
    "I'd like a little land" he says "not that I'd know what to do with it"

2. a fox got eight of our friend Polly's layers this week

(layers means hens)

last night her husband slept in a truck by the henhouse
to keep it away
kicked the tailgate at midnight when
the chickens started to squawk

it was a night flashing with storms in off the sea

today everyone talked of the lightning

last month a hawk got three of the midwives' hens

they have an office in town

3. here we ask "who did you see in town today?"

"who did you see at the co-op?"   it's always someone

my husband asks our daughter "did you see the midwives?"

4. last night the midwives were at a birth for a Baptist couple

I got the call at the office while on the other line talking about strawberry picking

he said "who's this?" and I said "who's this?"
and he said "are the midwives there?" and I said "no but I'm on the other line with one of them
is there a message?"
and he said
"um the message is the contractions are four minutes apart and steady"
then the flurry of love and rush of a birth

at the birth the mom started singing hymns at 9.5 cm
lay my burden down lord
and the midwife sang harmony

5. my husband talked about the house that called to him
 at men's group tonight
        just him and Chris and John
(they meet at the midwives' office)
        he rode his bike there in the dark

here is what the house has:
a soapstone sink
an old cook stove
a greenhouse
a guest cabin
exposed beams
2 acres
167 acres of preserved land
        it's in an eco homeowners association

we also saw a house in town and this is what it has:
painted wood floors
a copper bathtub
a trellised side porch

6. funny thing to "teach childbirth"
(which I teach):
        the body knows what it knows
the mind a black fog   a comic strip speech bubble
        gets in the way of the divine pictorial

so I traded
        "sit on the blow-up ball" &
            "crayon draw the labor you want"
for spinach, chard, a beautiful
head of bouncing lettuce with tiny slugs
        & two dozen pale blue & brown eggs
        three of them partially cracked
from the "expecting" couple who farm on Faerie Kingdom Road

When my sabbatical is over in 2010,
my family and I move back to Chicago
and, now tenured, I resume my job in academia,
thinking about whether or not to leave it
to live in Maine on one income (my husband's)
and be at home with my children while they are young.
While I make this decision,
my mother is dying of metastasized cancer in California.

I Return to the City

Someone poked a finger through the construction paper sky
and now I see God's face all the time, thick as cream,
and not just on midnight-centric holidays.
I don't consider it a gift.

Persistent bacterial infection from E.coli in the water
or repetitive stress fracture or vaccine injury.
I don't have any plans.
I don't see anyone on the weekends except all these strangers, all of whom smoke.

I used to write poems here.
I used to think I saw stars.
Now I've seen stars, write no more poems.
Buy twenty-five dollar tickets, plus the nine dollar and twenty cent convenience charge,
plus the three dollar retail outlet pickup charge,
for the concert that I hope will make me cry.
Say *this is one good thing about living in the city.*
Mean the band coming through to play the concert, not the paying. Not the crying.

I now think outer space is a real place.
That flora is real.
Somewhere else, air is what you can breathe, is what you choose.

The summer of the decomposing fetal rat
baited by poison at the bottom of the back stair.
The place where the girl texts whilst rollerblading in traffic.
The story of the donkey-kick break-in in the next tier:
The strangest I've ever seen, said the detective,
and he'd seen decapitations.
City of decapitations, of John Wayne Gacy.
Song of John Wayne Gacy on the album that makes me cry,
but the concert in this city sold out and now the tickets are one hundred dollars.

Is it the authentic we're after? asks my friend J.
Document it.
Up the iron, up the Vitamin D of which everyone, absolutely everyone,
is massively deficient, even the people in Southern California,
even though the best source is sunshine.

A bunch of homeschooling mothers here in Chicago are going to see *Eat Pray Love*.
Think about it. Document it. Don't go, though.

Call it *clarity* or call it foul.
A bad mood or chemical sensitivity.
On the spectrum.
A yellow bird dipped in soot.
Sea bird drowning in oil.

Weird oily residue in my mason jar of city tap water.

Daughter who earlier this summer picked strawberries in her own yard
says she is reading in a magazine about *outdoor thing-a-ma-jigs*.
Daughter says the giant American flag at the car dealership we pass
is one good thing about Chicago.

Are you someone who makes art during wartime?
Are you someone who does not make art during wartime?

In the country they put up enough food *for when the shit hits the fan*.
I used to disbelieve it. Now I'm back, and when it does,
you'll know where to find me.
I don't want a bull's eye on my scalp
and that handprint from *M* on my shoulder.

How do you live with love in a place you hate? In a place that feels like hate,
where all the strangers smoke on the street and the baby rat is still there, day after day?
How do you do it, God?

Thought to put something about recent flooding here but trying to refrain.

Neighbors

When I was last here, the building next door burned down,
and now that I'm back, the building next door has burned down.
The one on the other side. This life has a scraping sound.

I work in a tinderbox. I eat
from silver paper, talk about the toxic bottles.

It was sunny and cool all day and I missed it.
There were children today starting their schools
and I missed them. I missed them.
A day lost to freon, and no one in the hallway.
And generally, if you are generous, you are suspect.

There was a small spark over the song
about the serial killer. "That gets a high five":
the psychotic brain pulsing beneath a neighbor's floorboards.
Some of my workmates connected, loved each other over this.

It's a new year, a holy day,
and I spent it breaking soft little jokes into regrets.
Blinking silver into the cracks.

(I am an apple that glows when charged.)
(I risk my life.)
(I do not want to work in these ashes and roaches.)

Home is also a place where important things are said.
There are hundreds of others living today and taking this train away from our jobs—
one lent me the pen so I could write this.
He was surprised I asked him, surprised I said anything.
Let us all get home.

Lovely Day for a Wedding (and Panic)

Some peasants make good magic.
But my peasant stock made none except a golem:
what's plain in my blood is pessimism,
doomed&deserved and a big god
who is not a wheel.

When I married the Non, we had it done
by a tantric Buddhist hippie blueblood professor in Maine,
left the details wide,
and he appeared in white cotton gloves
to perform, he said, the trick:
transformation via witness, accompanied by silence
and all our friends dressed in sequins and bow ties
and holding brass bells on silk ribbons.
There were flowers we did not even pay for,
provided by the woman from the geodesic dome, Alda Stitch,
whom we've run into over and over ever since, like a witch.

All the Chicago kids in my classes are writing about god these days.
They convert and *de-*. They go to church.
They use titles like Sufjan uses titles,
Sufjan named after one major world religion
and grown up to sing and live through another.

One side effect of turning into a wife
is that I now weep from start to end of every rock show I attend.

I believe more and more in little white sugar pellets
with miniscule drops of poison in them held under the tongue.
In story medicine and Do Nothing medicine.
In the need for seasons and seeds.
In handwork and weeping.
In letting death come in its good hour (and I did not know
I'd believe this if I saw it, but I saw it, and I believed it).

In needs. In collectives of women making things.
In my marriage. In my marriage. Its consecration on that day.
This day. Its longness. Its shiny thread.

Oh what do I care of going out in the dark
to walk the dog in my nightgown?
My nightgown is fat white linen and a hundred years old.

Other Particular Strangers

My seatmate takes out a rough creamy envelope and pulls out a card of a pretty window IRELAND and a photograph slipped inside of a woman who looks like she could be my seatmate's mother cuddling a child who looks like he could be my seatmate's nephew? and studies this photo forever, as if it's a signifier, as if it's talking, and maybe it is, and when she slips it back in, her hands are shaky or maybe that's just the train.

Across the aisle a child throws her lollipop stick on the floor, litterer, and she is kind of a dirty child though her dimple is pretty. She puts her dirty pink hat on the woman next to her who is like a big still mountain, still but impatient. They get off at Belmont.

Somewhere a leaf falls. It's the highest mold count in five years. Somewhere it is not a city, unbelievably.

Before her semiotic photo, my seatmate was making magical gestures on her iPad.

In many places there are children, but not once I arrive at the office.

When my seatmate takes out her iPad again, I spy with my little eye that she has almost entered Peter's CaringBridge site. I was just sent a link to a CaringBridge site yesterday for my sister's rabbi's seven-year-old daughter Cara who has (unbelievably) a curable tumor. I first heard about CaringBridge from Rachel because of her doula trainer who died a death surrounded by loving. I almost entered Cara's CaringBridge site but did not verify and enter; I decided I could not enter the life of a seven-year-old girl I do not know with so much other caring I need to do. Was this cold, or connected? I do not know.

The pink hat woman has been replaced by a blonde in sunglasses reading *The Girl Who Played with Fire*. Everyone is.

What to make of CaringBridge when I want a real tiny bridge over a little creek and to bring lentil salad and muffins to those in need?

Now my seatmate is staring at a photo on her iPad and sighing and I am too shy to spy it: it could be of Peter, and Peter could be the boy in the IRELAND photo, and could be sick. My seatmate gets off at State and Lake so I will never know, never enter the life or death of that particular stranger.

When this train goes around the next bend, I will get off at Library.

Lyric I

From these two lips I own: the roots of rapture, oaken bones below a low looping path by the old stonewall, trailhead by the apple tree. I am blazed. There's the cairn. This me I am making, a maker of spells. Breaker. Binder. More in the kitchen, more time spent in barns, world-bleary, shop-worn, uniform of petticoat and mariner sweater.

And again—the dog? I forget her. She curls a blue corner under the cupboard of white powder pellets burst from their vials. I believe more in the disease than the cure. I consider the pox party. I keep my dead, keep them close for awhile afterward.

I go the fairground and weep at the worksong, dance with my farmer. I heart my farmers. The roots of this suffix in pasture and lyrics. More like the moors now, green rocky roads, gray rocky shore. I lie back most afternoons and think of England.

And will I get a job? I will go pick apples. You can tell by the crown the name of the varietal. Me, I'm not sure. The tip of my nose is flesh, a sow's. The harrow and the plough. The hoe and the hearth. My hand with the heart drawn inside it. The breeze on the cows. And gas, and guzzle, and ghazal—I am named for a play of an ill wind, or a mermaid or fey, but my knees are real dirty.

Diamond Joe, they sang. Roll on. A low tone. Godspeed. I don't know. I think I'm at ease.

Or, Down the Rabbit Hole

My job is to raise a violet flicker in the charming youth.

No, my job is to lick down bits of their stray hair,
        get called *Maman*, be snarked at and doubted and asked for guidance.

My job is the forms in the self-addressed, stamped envelopes provided.

My job is to singe my hems a bit, out of office (and official) loneliness.

My job is to use a whiteboard, and sticky notes, and to print out the class list.

My job has been partially redacted.

My job is blurry, infinite, permanent, tenured and tenuous.

My job is to come up with a way to teach a course about something that drives me to distraction
        but that could also be relevant to the interests of the youth.

My job is to act like something that is both very important and very unimportant—my job,
        and the field in which my job exists—is both very important and very unimportant.

My job is to pull on my cowgirl boots.

My job is to gladly have tea with youth who have grown up but still believe that this is my job.

My job is to figure out when to care deeply and when to be cavalier,
        and when to act the opposite of what I'm really feeling.

My job is to bring a little bit of pasta salad in a reusable stainless steel container and eat
        while I'm talking about the male gaze.

My job is to enact the look of surprise on the face of the bear at the edge of the suburbs
        in the photograph the gracious youth keep bringing in to class.

My job is to explain what purpose the uterus serves,
        and what purpose the *Gothic Mode*,
        and what purpose eating out of stainless steel containers and drinking out of glass jars,
        and why Emily Dickinson will win the thumb-wrestle of lyric motif any day.

My job is to keep bringing up wrestling.

My job is to keep bringing up wrestling,
        and to spell the author's last name on the board
        so that the delightful youth will find it when they do not go to the library
        and do not go to the bookstore.

My job is to make sure my skirt is not tucked into the top of my underwear
        when I return from the bathroom after break.

My job is to organize a James Spader movie marathon:
    Pretty in Pink, *Sex Lies & Videotape*, and *Secretary*,
    none of which the youth have seen.
    (They have never seen any John Hughes movies.)

My job is to order the A/V equipment through the online form.

My job is to look for signposts about God.

My job is to talk about *wrestling*, and *risking*, and *challenging*, and *struggling*
        so often that the youth want to take me down.

My job is to therefore believe in the transmogrifying effect of Thanksgiving break.

My job is to go home and make vegetable fried rice for dinner with the family.

My job is to first wipe the dog hair out of the wok.

My job is to grate the fresh ginger directly into my left eye.

My job is not to think about my job while making dinner.

My job is to leave dinner cooking on the stove for a few minutes
        while I go kiss my daughter goodnight.

My job is not to think about my job while going to kiss my daughter goodnight.

My job is to try not to weep every time I remember that the youth
        have never read *Alice's Adventures in Wonderland*.
        They have only seen the Disney movie version.

Gifts

I'm trying to buy you another life for the holiday by buying you a cologne named after a state and packaged in a tiny amber bottle which itself represents this other life, because we've made that treacherous mistake of conflation like how campfire smoke smells like a flannel blanket which is maybe the smell of tree sap or new breath and this is the dusty magic of cologne that makes it a popular and expensive holiday gift, this confusion, this gesture at memory and this reliance on gold-flecked flaw but I'm trying to buy you a purple flannel cloud of deep sleep which I know you want and I'm trying to buy a crystal hung inside a carved wooden sun as a symbol of our dead boy on the year he would have been three but I am unclear if I am trying to make anybody cry with these gifts.

NOTHING IN NATURE IS SAFER THAN NOTHING

in conversation with Julie Carr's *100 Notes on Violence*

1.

Another thing that happened in the community in Maine I keep saying
and saying I want to live in:

A house with a man with many shrines, gun by the bed,
woman and child,
woman raped, child cowering,
a nice red velvet cake of a front room for the man to watch tv with the shrines,
a back little dark room for woman and child
like a bunker where he kept them.

He kept them.

Shrines with Hitler's own silverware
(the man had family money from his family),
plans for dirty bombs, chemicals in the woman's kitchen sink.

He kept uranium, thorium, lithium metal,
thermite, aluminum powder, beryllium, boron.
Black iron oxide and magnesium in the house.

A growing obsession with child pornography.

White white man, slept with a gun.

And wash-brained woman and wash-brained child sleeping with fear
in their bunker rooms,
and no friends, no school, no outside life outside the house,
no phone calls from family (they thought she was dead,
thought he'd for sure killed her years before)
and he slept with a gun every night.

2.

On the El train where I start to think of this while reading Julie's book
I feel everyone's nicotine in me, killing my nice clear parts.

Two seats away that man's or that man's nicotine clots me
so I zip my slippery gray puff coat over my nose and hide my breath inside
but the nicotine gets in anyway, gets into my stomach through my lungs, I can feel it,
everyone's everpresent city cigarette still on their bodies and in their breath
and now on mine, in mine
so I move to the other side of the car
and breathe and notice the man I'm now sitting next to has nicotine on him, too,
and now it's in my sinus passages, my polyps, the back of my hair, in my kitchen.

When I get off the train and step outside into the night,
everyone around me lights up.

Oh everyone's got a hoodie a hoodie a hoodie on
everyone's got a hoodie on to protect their cigarettes from the cold.

3.

COMMUNE (a hippie place to live, with bare feet)
COMMUNE (be with)
COMMUNE (with nature)

UNITY

Also, COMMON. I like that one, too.

4.

When the woman thought the white man in the house was going to start going after the child (girl child)
because of his growing obsession with child pornography and the girl getting older,
the woman found a night that was for going to the man's bed while he slept
and taking a gun that was there and killing him.

The gun was a Colt 45 Peacemaker pistol.

5.

One woman in the city today said this to me:
            Are you going to DC for AWP? I'm not going to DC for AWP: bedbugs! All the hotels have bedbugs! One woman I work with got bedbugs from a hotel and had to move twice; her family, she had a family; had to leave behind grandmother's special things, things you can't replace; you can check the beds but they get in the picture frames, in the cracks; one person came home with them and opened up her suitcase and her whole bathroom was infested; they have to melt your appliances, rewire everything, move again; they were eating her children!; in Cincinnati people are sleeping on the street I mean choosing to move out onto the hard street; I'm not going.

This woman nearly died in a car accident when she was young,
was possibly beaten by her parents when young,
had drug dealer boyfriend, got punched, saw shots,
hates crack-down farm where she came from,
and *she's* not going because of the bedbugs.
That's how serious shit is with bedbugs.
They can ruin your life.

6.

When the woman and child went to the courthouse afterward
the child saw a black man and started shrieking and ran to a corner of the hall and cowered.
She thought he was the devil because of what her white man father had taught her.
This was the first black man she'd ever seen.

           It took a long time to make the white white brainwash start to—

7.

Reading Julie's book on the El train in the city with a very high homicide rate
I think, *This book is about violence everywhere because Julie's in Colorado. Because it's Colorado.*
People seem in touch with their guns and their clots there.
It's the state, I think.
As if it's the state.

So I'm writing this to say that yes, people have guns everywhere,
I know people with guns in the community in Maine,
I am friends with people with guns in the community in Maine
(I do not know myself to be friends with people with guns in Chicago),
but yes, I once saw anti-Semitic flyers up at the Food Co-op,
and people smoke everywhere, there are cigarettes on all the sidewalks,
in small towns in Maine, too, yes yes.

But please I want to be at Polly's farm next winter for the bee
where me and other mothers will cut out the little windows on her handmade advent calendars
and eat molasses cookies and make a peaceful union with the dark days of the year.

Please.

8.

REWIRE

9.

Chicago goes 6 days without a homicide

Tracy Swartz posted Jan. 27, 2011 at 7:00 a.m. | no comments

A 49-year-old man was found beaten to death Monday in Morgan Park, marking the community area's first homicide this year, a RedEye analysis of preliminary police data found.

The death also was the only homicide in the last week, from Jan. 19 through Wednesday afternoon, RedEye determined. RedEye has never published a homicide map with just one victim since the newspaper began printing homicide maps in February 2009.

10.

The white man lived up the street from us,
with woman and child,
in a house a few blocks away from the house we lived in,
with his Hitler silverware.
(A small town,
so small everything that happens in town is a few blocks away.)
No one knew what he kept in there.
I didn't know.

11.

Another woman in the city with me today said:
    I'm good, I'm good
    Good I got that divorce
        got rid of that womanizer
    Good I stopped abusing those substances
    Good I stopped getting cracked on capoeira
        that shit can be like crack

12.

But also in that small town in Maine when they cracked the woman and child from the house after she killed the man, all these strangers came to the trial and stood for her and stood with her and hugged her when she passed in and out of the courtroom and didn't know her but were with her. A general call went out from some women who lived a few blocks away from me. I got it by email. Come and stand with her. And people did, mostly women, to wear stickers that said FREE the woman, to light up around her, to say, even though he was sleeping and even though it was murder she is not a criminal, she was trying to get free, it was self-defense for the years of rape and guns and Nazi silverware and uranium in the kitchen sink, it was trying to save her girl child, she turned herself in, she should be free, she should be finally finally finally free.

And the judge did. He let her be free.

13.

What I'm saying is I want COMMUNITY
with my breath and with Polly's advent bee
and with freedom and the women who stand with it
and friends who grow food and haul water,
and friends with guns, too (Joanne said she'll take me hunting),
and bare feet, too,
and that feels safe to me, though I know there are no guarantees anywhere.

Community: I am using the word so much
you think I'd be sick of it
but I will not stop.

Note to self:

When the semester is over, remember to write a poem about the "welcome back"/"we hate you" dinner held for you by your colleagues upon your return from sabbatical where, under the guise of celebrating your return, they leveled all their complaints against you then decided it was probably best if we all went dutch.

Instead of "Poet of Place"

maybe Poet of Academic Job Market:
I live where I landed, where the job felled me, and adopted it openly

Middlingwestern by birth and by paycheck
Lake person, mud person
         A skyline stuck in a stone

I've been regionless, adaptable
born in the corn but grew up in the woods
grew up in the woods but all my family's from the city
left that city long ago but it's still in the pace of my speech, my footfall

How'd you come by that big cheesy smile anyway, you ask me?
         I live in a billboard

Went from a city resembling nothing less than an apple
where I wrote about what happened in other people's lower windows

to shit city
where I made games and little books and finally love

to itty city
where the coffee shops never opened and mostly I couldn't find a friend
or a quality chocolate chip cookie and marked papers and time and ran up hills

and then I went to heaven
in a cabin for a five-week fellowship
where they bring you soup and a big hunk of bread in a basket silently at noon
and I wrote about foxes and Jews

and then I went on the market

and I almost went to the insurance town with the small museum

and I almost went to roll tide

and I almost went to a rainy place with politics under grow lamps

but instead I got the job in the broad landlocked city of big portions

Are the poems here flatter? greater?
more bronzed? more presidential?
more elevated? Polish? Irish?
marshaled? fielded?

I'm open-ended

I ended up here

with little rigor or reason
but more chiming, via the United C Concourse tunnel at O'Hare

I'm in the middle, in the muddle
        indeterminate

I own no land, not a square of soil to hold or sow or turn
City-feeder, bottom-dweller

I'm gonna get a new job making teeny tiny sculptures out of dollhouse chairs
for post office plazas and other enormous public spaces

Go back.

For myself, I'm waiting

out the dead days, relieved to feel dull,

but hungry for a wooden ornament

buried under a pile of fir.

This is turning out to be a California Christmas:

pink-green, and twilighty.

It undoes a woman who wants to move

where she wants to for the trees

or strangers. If I believe this,

I am duller than I thought,

which is entirely possible.

        today is the last day I probably saw my mother alive
            which is a sentence I can't figure out how to write—
        I can write it this way though she is not dead
            but if it's the last time I will see her then—
                she is not dead—
            and is in hospice care so it is pretty safe to say—

on the plane home they show a free movie I choose to watch because it has moods in it,
    and a burial, and a man with a beard, and Sissy Spacek in a cloche—
      it's fall in the movie, or maybe spring, though today is the winter solstice,
          darkest of the year,
    and three years ago today I buried my second child in the woods in Maine—
      you know what they say about threes—

      and my mother who hardly spoke when I saw her this time
        which is probably the last time—
      but once to say "I am quiet not a lot so take advantage of it"—
      her syntax too unraveling but for her because of the painkillers
        or the brain tumors—
      but she did speak a few times and of those times many
        which in the case of this visit means "two times"
              were about my hair—

    the woods were so frozen and snowed that day
    and we pulled the tiny wooden coffin on a little sled—

            is your hair soaking earlier? she said—
    she was a mantis version of my mother, on spindles—
        a specter—
          lidless, overlidded, extraterrestrial—

the movie begins with a house on fire, burning from within, and shotguns,
                          and wool, and a boy vomiting—
    the man wants to buy his own funeral and is told *you can't buy forgiveness*
        it's free but you have to ask for it
is asked *are you ready for the next life?*—

I am not writing here though about my long estrangement from my difficult mother who is dying—
  it turns out the movie I have chosen to watch on the plane home from seeing my mother
           is a movie about death which I didn't know—

would the phrase "step on it" have come into use so soon after people started driving cars?—

and would people in a small town in maybe Missouri in the 30s have so easily and swiftly
        alienated themselves from shotguns and splitting wood and mules
            as to be put off by the bearded man who lives in the woods?—
                        no, sir, I don't think so—

and did I tell you how she smelled, like a cavemouth, rank and loamy?—

            somebody does a wrong and dies anyway—

    *there's alive and there's dead and there's somewhere in between them
            that I hope you never know anything about* the old man says
    to the young father with a baby in the movie I have chosen to watch on the plane
        going back to my family from seeing my mother, family of origin—
            not writing here about how my home in Chicago has not felt like home
                since we buried the baby in the wooly dark woods of Maine—

I am pretty sure they did not say "watch and learn" or "I am out of here" in the 30s—

and what if there is a contradance in the movie, and a mason jar of hard cider?—
                        a skillet of rabbit cooked in butter?—
            I am a person who is now looking everywhere for meaning—

            I am going to try and tell it—
        to ask forgiveness of the person who deserves it,
                not God (though maybe also)—
it turns out the thing you have to say might be a house burning through its windows—
hair like chains, so heavy to carry around all day long—
                            right and wrong all tangled up—
        the story you finally tell after forty years is broken down, is ash in the mouth—

"what will you write about this time, on the long ride home?" RZ asked—
            how I offered her my own milk to drink as maybe one of her last drinks
                    but she was only confused,
                laughed a little, and I poured the strange little hope of a gift
                        down the kitchen sink—

            "you are going to a place I've never been
    and I am watching how you get there and how you come back" RZ said—

                              his ghost-love comes walking out of the woods—
                    I wish you peace from the burden of your heart and mind,
                              I wish it for us all—
so it turns out it's a movie about a burial
on the exact day of the third anniversary of my son's burial
            and you know what they say about threes—

                    when I leave my mother's house my face is more beautiful, newer,
                after having spent those hours looking at her breathing,
        looking at the bone in the middle of her nose, her face vacant of fat or color,
                        tuned tight to the skull,
        the long dark hairs by her mouth, the fetal eyes, the too-square teeth—
                    the sickness eating along her spine—

at the airport everyone is bringing their girlfriends home for the holiday,
    girlfriends in high heels and novelty elf hats and more makeup than I think they need—

            the cab driver bringing me home from O'Hare at midnight has a tv screen
                        selling ads and trivia—

it is so so hard to find some silence and some still in this life—
    how did we get here, to this way of being?—
        and I don't think I'm kidding myself that it'd be easier if we lived in Maine again—

        the cab driver tells me to turn off the light but I tell him I am writing
                                and he thinks I said I am reading—

            I think the Dalai Lama said it's hard to practice meditation if you live in a city—
                    but I could be kidding myself—

I tried to be still and silent with her, to listen to my breath but found myself
listening to her breath and rationalized this as okay,
as compassion and genuine witness—
            but do maybe wish I'd sat still with her longer, more than the hours I did—
                it was so much like a birth with the waiting and the Chux pads,
                    the slow painful trips to the toilet and back—
                which is part of the reason I wanted to give her my milk—
                which seems to be the part of the story I most want to tell—
                    this and the things she said about my hair—

in the cab all the trivia is oddly about Boston though we are in Chicago and for a moment
   I think I have taken a plane to the wrong home, a city I lived in before I had children
                that never felt like home—

I am not writing here about how more than anything
I want to live in a place with woods,
      not in a city any longer—

          turns out the cab driver's meter had genuinely turned off
              and at my curb he is willing to take whatever I offer—
    so much unsuspected kindness in the nighttime, really—
I am writing in the middle of the night on the darkest day of the year,
      on the winter solstice on which three years ago I buried my second of three children
           and on which this year I saw my mother for maybe the last time—
        I am reading absolutely everything in the world as a lesson and a talisman—

I was reading an article

Julia Butterfly Hill now older   old as me now

saying *They cut Luna down   Now I call her Flattie*

and in the accompanying photograph a stump

coffee table wide and sleek on the forest floor with Julia behind

and arrayed with my recently dead mother's painted gourd ducks

which were turtles in their marked shells

all manner of totem creatures   companion species

and I said to my sister *These were hers These were not hers*

it was a grave site

"Sitting Around Singing Kumbaya"

As I was putting the baby down for his nap today, singing him Kumbaya—

which is rumored to be a Gullah phrase meaning "come over"—

the Gullah people descendents of West Africans enslaved and brought to this country—

having come over and not having wanted to come over—

I thought about how people use the phrase "sitting around singing Kumbaya"
to mean something you would never want to be caught doing—

something stupid and idealistic and futile—

the song Kumbaya whose origin and meaning is still debated and partially erased—

I think of sand and sea here, history under sand and lost at sea—

but one thing that is known is that Kumbaya is a song well-meaning white folk revivalists
"borrowed" from the Gullah people—

"borrowed" a word which, when used by well-meaning white folks, often means "stolen"—

from the Gullah whose descendents had stayed
on the Sea Islands of South Carolina and Georgia
and kept a way of life, kept a language, kept their ways on the islands off the mainland—

kept a way with walking sticks and with rice and with stories—

with language that is English and Creole and Sierra Leone Krio—

the Gullah people who sang a spiritual about trouble in mind, trouble in mind
called "Kumbaya" that was perhaps a plea to God to pay attention and *come over here, Lord—*

a song which was first caught by a white guy—

a former English professor, a folklore buff—

(someone kind of like me, really, I think, putting the baby to sleep—)

a white man who recorded the song, trying to keep it for history and culture—

but maybe this is a kind of stealing, too—

a kind of enslaving—

how "well meaning" often means "fucked up"
and is most often associated with liberal white folks like me—
if my meaning is even well at all, which I sometimes doubt—

and how the white folk revivalists, many of whom did after all march with Dr. King
and with union workers and got arrested and got blacklisted—

brought the song out off the islands and into the world—

and Kumbaya became a song sung at Civil Rights marches—

and later sung at summer camps,
probably introduced by well-meaning white folk hippie camp counselors who had marched—

so that now the folk song, the spiritual Kumbaya—

whose meaning is disputed but maybe means "come by here"—

is associated with little children and hippies—

and thus thought of as weak-minded and boring and worthy of ridicule—

because we live in a culture where things associated with children are thought of as idiotic—

so that "sitting around singing Kumbaya" is a shorthand meaning
wasting our time or not getting done what needs to get done—

or something absolutely inane and powerless—

in which people are required to *compromise* or *find common ground*—

so that now the phrase "singing Kumbaya," a song once sung for peace and justice,
is used to steal the power of people who work for peace and justice—

how U.S. Ambassador John Bolton said sarcastically that he was surprised that a farewell dinner
for then-United Nations president Kofi Annan did not end in the singing of Kumbaya—

and Republicans said that Barack Obama, our first Black president,
was maybe just singing Kumbaya with his ideas for massive health care reform—

but during his election Obama himself said,
"The politics of hope is not about holding hands and singing 'Kumbaya'"—

he who, like all of us, ought to have maybe spent more time in college
doing folk culture research—

and I think about the Gullah people keeping their culture through and despite and after
years of enslavement, and displacement, and colonization—

and singing, according to the various scholarly interpretations
of the meaning of the song Kumbaya—

"come over here to this place where we keep what is ours—
bear witness to it, how we have kept it alive"—

or, "come over here and stand with us, if you mean so well"—

or, singing to God, "do not forsake us, we who are suffering so mightily"—

Kumbaya, a song of peace and justice, a song to be sung in the streets—

and then I think, as I put the baby to sleep, singing Kumbaya,
about how I think *sitting around singing Kumbaya*—

singing, in a circle, in a group, the open, arousing song of former slaves in a language
no one can quite trace, a language risen hot fire from ashes of all that was stolen—

is perhaps one of the most notable and useful things I can think of doing—

and that even the song being sung by children at summer camp
or well-meaning white folks in coffee houses is a lot less stupid than making war—

"making war" itself a phrase associated with hippies
as if one could simply choose instead to "make love"—

an idea, a slogan which seems to have fallen so far out of fashion—

so I am aware that I myself sound like a hippie, really am basically just a hippie—

if "just" a hippie means someone who, yes, would rather see children run barefoot in grass and languages invented and songs sung than wars mongered—

that I am someone, well-meaning or not,
who wants to hold hands and sing Kumbaya in a circle—

that singing anything in a circle of folks, really, as a group, is all I want from this life—

Three Pear Trees: First Poem of the New Year, 2011

I have a strong request that the soundtrack to the world
include more handclaps, please.

I have a feeling that if the two books of poems I am writing could leave my house
and go into the world, maybe I'd write poems that tried to be really friendly, like
Hello there! or a psychedelic healing vision.

Last night I dreamed my ex-boyfriend's mother
was showing me her home and her lawn and she had almost a full acre
and on the front lawn there were three pear trees in full bloom
and it was the most beautiful and lush thing I'd ever seen,
and then I realized it was a time of winter and only a few trees around were blooming
but all of her trees were.

My ex-boyfriend's mother is dead.

This is the time of year for dead people,
and for the birthdays of very close sisters and children,
and I myself am getting a little closer to dying all the time.

I would hug this condition if I could.

I'd like to share this dream and this condition in a circle with you,
maybe in something that resembles a church.
I would like Hoa to read my I Ching again
and to learn to do the nettle infusions.
I would like to learn to hypnotize myself to go without income for awhile.
I want to get a double rain storm cover for the kids' stroller
so we could stroll through the winter and through all the double storms.

I dreamt my friend from high school with the very small body
was pregnant and I helped her with the birth.

I am torn between wanting to meet you at the church
for a morning of silent prayer or a morning of Jungian dream analysis
or a morning talking about generating compassion,
but I know I'd like to meet you Sunday mornings.
I would like those handclaps to come in about now.

Dollars, and The Change

I need maybe 5000 maybe 10000 maybe 8000 dollars a year from part time work
but what   maybe teaching   maybe birthwork, lactation or postpartum
                      maybe teaching about birth
and but why   for clothes or food or to feel like I'm not letting anyone down,
                                                                          self / self / self

and but which part of myself do I sell and which to keep

and but by need I also mean I want to replace a new fiberglass tub
with a very old porcelain over cast iron tub
a perfectly good new laminate kitchen countertop
with some old and hard-to-care-for locally-sourced soapstone

I think every room should have something over 100 years old in it
for a sense of history and ancestry
and so no one will build a new bed just for me with new materials
and this takes what I estimate at 5000 to 25000 dollars a year
as a blanket of not worrying about buying the older maybe better maybe more expensive things
instead of the newer cheaper things

takes money to not think about it

what do you know about insulated flooring options?
what do you know about vapor barriers?

when I'm in the snow, it's enough to just be in the snow
when I'm sitting on a rock in the Atlantic ocean, it's enough
when I'm bathing in the walking in some woods I don't know well,
I need 0 dollars per year to know who I am

or we'll see
we'll see about that, missy

though I did get in a kayak last summer and made it all the way across the pond
and you know I loved it even with those dastardly enormous water spiders
pinned along the surface
was good at it

when I'm surrounded by water, under water swimming
I sing to myself
do you do that?

I only want to speak with my mouth full of snow

        maybe then I won't make all these ridiculous pronouncements, predictions

all my friends and I are older now, 40ish
we look it
we look it in the face
I'm mostly proud about it

three of my friends this month including me had cycles four days longer than usual
and maybe that's next, what's coming

        the change

I want to look things in the face
                        self /

go with the upside-down mountain that goes down down down into the ground

I need maybe 1500 dollars a year from teaching women about the power of their labors
and their breastmilk
I can also trade this labor for moo milk in a glass jar
        because some of these women keep family cows

when I was 17 all I wanted was to grow up and be someone who could buy milk in a glass jar
without worrying about it, without thinking about
but as an aesthetic and health and consumer and political choice
so in a way with thinking about it fully, facing it
but doing it anyway, freely
and I've now become that person who buys that glass jar milk

I want
a positive capacity for emptiness

all roads continue to lead to Keats
and all roads continue to be the ones Thoreau walked on
and lately all my roads lead to Sonia Sanchez too

who was in the taxicab line behind me and Rachel in DC
so we shared one and asked her to tell us things and she told us
Academe kills women
and
Be in your bodies. Women are not taught how to be in our bodies

then five days later came to my school in Chicago and talked about SNCC
and Martin and Malcolm

and I cried and cried

I was trying to leave for work this morning when Seth Bournival called
to talk about the new old house I'm buying
suggested local white pine simply laid over the vinyl
suggested Bioshield, a non-toxic sealant (he's been very pleased with the results)
and agreed that slate would be best for the 5 foot walkway
from garage to mudroom through the home office
and recommended two southern-facing windows punched through to the yard
I was almost late for work
I was in a practical swoon
I felt practical and adult and sick and swoony
it would take maybe 14000 dollars maybe 21000 dollars
for the pine and the mud and the southern light

have no idea how to end this poem because it's a circle
like the poem about visiting my mother who was dying

just put a big fat circle in it for the empty place
        and the mouth with her questions and the eyes with her coins

Two Fat Braids Crossed at the Crown

       Mishearing you holding out the gadget plug,
I joke *Dis cord*?

       Yes, I'd like a little more in general
though not in the delicious sinkhole of our seven-year marriage.

       I'm talking about a counterculture.

       I'm nearly forty.
I've only recently figured out how to fix my hair
(two fat braids crossed at the crown)
and with what (coconut oil melted in its glass jar on the radiator,
rosemary or apricot oil if the ends are really thirsty).

       In my 20s my 45-year-old boyfriend told me stories about the '60s,
his lover who wore Victorian camisoles that made cars screech to a halt as she crossed the street.
You could get Victorian whites in the thrift stores then,
it was like 50s overcoats to us now, stodgy furs yearning
to become bohemian on some rosy shoulders.
He also told me about sleeping in French graveyards and wearing a velvet blazer
to the Fillmore East: those were things you could do then, things I missed.

       Once married and nearly forty and the mother of people,
how much time can you devote to subversion? Or to porn?

       I can hear you in the bathroom with the _____.

       We are pets.

       I want to be foxier, a white buffalo child-woman like the old hippie named me
when I was working in the food co-op during grad school.
All those lushly empty hours spent dunking heads of lettuce in ice water in steel sinks,
or running up and down hills in the snow fantasizing about childbirth,
or hitting the snooze button for hours while listening to the BBC World Service.

       I am trying to be friendly.

       I am trying to be more connected than correcting.

      I am trying to remember to kiss you at least once a day in a surprising manner
but it's surprisingly hard.
Really, any manner would be surprising, because mostly I kiss the baby,
who was born ugly—purple and hairless and skinny—
but has lured me by now into a wholly irrational devotion,
a kind of mesmer. I say awful things to him—
who loves you so much? pretty pretty pretty?—
and he holds me by my braids,
wants me to rub him across the face with my hair.

      This is my affair with your son, who looks quite like the best of your father sometimes,
who died this time of year when I was pregnant with this baby,
and the police called you from Ohio and I brought the phone to where you were
breaking down boxes in the basement of our newly rented house overlooking the sea,
and then you had to go and be kin.

      My whole life I have wanted to wear history on my body
and politics and books on my face.
Soon my face will be too old to be blank enough to carry any other message than its own.

Flying into the Nation's Capital to Test My Mettle as Some Chattel

      everybody gets a car!
on the airport tv Oprah is jumping up + down + screaming

      so it *is* about stuff after all

      the poor know there's no romance in poverty
+ this is America after all

      mostly I'm worried about leaving my house
+ sleeping with the bedbugs
have a plan to keep the lights on all night

      but my body is an unlit place
a deep ego pit
better bring Pema Chodron book in my personal carry-on item

      a guy in front of me has an arrowhead tattoo on the back of his neck

      we are halfway to spring
feast of Brigid
goddess of poetry + midwifery
two things I love so I guess the pagans do have the last say
may become one of them

      I am trying to be uncynical
I am trying to be a force of nature, a thunderbird overhead
but even the thunderbirds look ironic on all the cheapest t-shirts and tattoos
the fake plastic turquoise

      the people of the People's Temple in its early days
say it was the real thing
it was Love
Jim Jones himself was kind + generous

maybe it was the speed or power
but I just read about the vats + the children injected with the liquid or having it poured over them
+ the screaming, caught on tape

      I feel so sick
I have to throw the whole article directly into the garbage
I vow I will never make a joke about drinking Kool-Aid again
but I probably won't keep it

      I vow I will be a thunderbird

      I do want to get a car
I'm talking to Rich about the 84 Benz converted to run on Straight Vegetable Oil
but you have to start + finish up with a flush of diesel

      the self is a cave

      but there's a flicker
there's a molten core

      I need to shake off the massacre
or be with the massacre
+ the juiced children

      + the current revolution in Egypt

      I want to love all these people
as we travel into the air
into the capital where the Pentagon is back on the ground

Poem About Nothing

for Rachel, again

1. I don't want to write a poem about nothing. I'm finding it very hard to write one when my child is in a flannel-sheeted pile at my back and another child has my right breast arrayed into his mouth and another child has died and stands in the corner of the room in the form of an altar.

It's difficult to write a poem about nothing when the air could smell like rocket if only I took the time to grow rocket, nother word for arugula. Hard to write about nothing when oil drilling.

Or the African-American woman with the white and orange microbraids who on the train last night was cursing out that man about weed while pushing back her toddler into the plastic umbrella stroller, and then when the man left she kissed her daughter's face and cleaned her tenderly with her thumbs. They can't all fit into a poem about nothing.

Nor can how I wept to see her and the toddler in such distress and thought about the One Right Path and how to intervene and was weeping so mightily the white woman next to me asked about *me*, not the other mom.

2. Sometimes people enjoy poems about nothing.

I'd like to write enjoyable poems.

I am thinking about writing poems about sex.

But they will probably still not be that enjoyable. They will probably have oil drilling in them.

3. also what if you are trying to respond to the music of joints and thoughts? *not a poem about nothing but close. can't even remember what I meant when I wrote this: drugs? music? community, again?*

4. Childless people can be said to have the privilege to choose to write about nothing. There, I said it. I *forefronted maternity* again, without *transcending* it. But don't some childless people write about nothing sometimes? Does it take enormous effort? And all those childless people were children, once: they have mothers. I do not want to read every single person's poems about their mothers though I don't not want to read those poems.

This poem was supposed to have three more parts in it: one about war, one about whiteness, and one about money. You can imagine them here:

—Feb 11, 2011 & Feb 17, 2012

Dear Robyn Gabel, State Representative, 18th District, Illinois,

I've been meaning to write to you for awhile, to tell you how grateful I am to you for your co-sponsorship work on behalf of a bill to legalize Certified Professional Midwives (CPMs) in the state of Illinois, a bill which would have provided access for women who, like me, chose to birth their children at home with skilled professionals trained in the art and science of natural childbirth. A bill I've been working toward myself, in various ways, for some years now. A bill that was defeated. I am proud and thankful to live in a district where my representative was a key co-sponsor to this bill.

Birthing my children at home changed my life in ways both tangible and spiritual. Having to fight political battles in order to have the right to birth my children at home with CPMs changed my life, too. And having these children has changed my life, in a million, billion ways. I think you might be a mother, too—you have done so much work on behalf of keeping families healthy—and I feel sure you understand.

One way my life has changed since having children is that I feel an even more urgent sense to keep our planet habitable for all beings, all life. I want the mountains and the forests and the deserts and the plains to exist when I try to visit them with my children in the coming years. I want plants and animals and insects and birds to exist so that my children can learn their names. Of course, I also want all of these things for reasons that have nothing to do with my own children. But my own children bring these issues home for me.

This is a poem about off-shore drilling. I wish I were more informed about off-shore drilling, frankly. Here's what I know: I know I don't want it to happen. I know that it means destroying the lives and ecosystems of untold sentient beings, and I know I want no part of that killing. I also know that it's being done to feed an oil-driven economy, and that an oil-driven economy will be the end of us if we don't cut it out. (I wanted to put an expletive in the previous sentence, but I won't, because I am hoping you will take this at least somewhat seriously.) I know that I think it would be a very good idea if Americans were forced—quite literally, forced! Required! By law!—to use far, far less oil than we currently use. Refusing to drill off-shore seems one reasonable way to help us come into contact with oil independence, which will have to be our future if we want a future.

I think here again of my children.

The mission behind this poem is to participate in a project in which poets ask our government representatives to "control Big Oil." It occurs to me that the notion of controlling nearly anything about my own life or the lives of my children is a notion of which I am deeply suspicious, and a notion that torments me. But it also occurs to me that some individuals, some institutions can exert some control over some things—democratic laws and governments and legislative bodies and corporations, to name a few. So: you could do this. You could help our country be a place that tries to honor and protect the earth we live on, that tries to limit the environmental damage done by companies.

It further occurs to me that you could do this by being part of a community: our government. Our government can be a community! That's a beautiful thought.

There's a book, you've probably heard of it, called *Last Child in the Woods*. Well, I refuse to have my children be the last children in the woods. In fact, I am moving my children and my family out of your district and the state you represent in order to live in a place with a lot more woods, and I plan to spend a lot more time in future years being in the woods with my children. So I need there to be woods in the world. So I need reduced, not increased, oil production and usage.

I hope this doesn't lessen the impact of anything I've said here. To state the obvious, refusing to allow new or expand existing oil-drilling projects or support reckless endangerment of our planet and our habitats are both local and global issues, and they go far beyond Evanston, Illinois. But they can happen in Evanston, Illinois, too. Everything has to happen somewhere.

I'd like to read this poem to you in person but I have very little time these days, largely because of these young children I keep talking about, so I'm sending it to you instead.

And yes, this is a poem. When I was working on the homebirth legislation, I was instructed by wise, well-informed activists not to write letters like this when meeting with my representatives, not to stray from the party line or from the key points. It feels something of a radical act to write in the way I most want to write, to a person in your position, a position of legislative power. So that's what makes it a poem, to me.

With love (yes, love),

Arielle Greenberg
Evanston, IL

By the door is a small woven basket on the floor
and I take my credentials out of my back pocket
and drop them inside.

Now I can step through.

On the other side is a succulent emptiness.

On the other side I am wearing my work pants.

I smell like roots, like soup.

I think I know everything, and I know I am wrong.

When You Feel like Crying at a Faculty Meeting

A job is what you can hold in the palm of your hand—

    here, son, a plot of land, a lamb in its wool

You can ball it up

    It can ball you up

(a cut star said it another way)

    so we are packing boxes   I am leaving leaving leaving

Handcuffs of velvet, handcuffs of gold

    Feeling my water

Putting on my silver (like Joni in "Carey")

    A rounder tree said *you are* going toward, *not* running away

A terror is what I hold behind my left shoulderblade where there could be a vestigial wing, hurt I was born with

    A *secure job* is a body memory

A voting bloc is not a community, either

    They are making proposals and I'm writing this down

Even so I'm paying more attention than the one in the corner who *cannot comply*

    No one is getting married today

Are my teeth just chattering?

    How many dollars for less time *outside the home*?

And what work will I do what work will I do what work will I do

    Really means money

Is the job in the field?

       You know I think yes I am going toward more working in a field

Green grass, lamb—oh let's not with the pastoral

       But it's there   it's open

A completely unlocked unknowing

A Way Out

I want to take a vow of chastity: to write only toward what I don't know

If I come to know something, I should allow it to be divine and not speak of it

A dream while in Maine of seeing huge clouds made of millions of small stones
gathering and hovering above the ocean at the horizon, moving toward shore

An inevitable apocalypse we are powerless to stop, know nothing about, can only see coming

      (the horizon is just my perspective)

Also some sense of this being what I think foolishly that I can escape: clusters of black doom

In the dream it seems both inescapable and that I have indeed found a way out

Have I found a way out

Door made of stones, door in the stone wall

My mind is the black box that contains the ticker tape key to my dissatisfaction
The recording of my unease

      All at once I feel the stone wall in my stomach
      To place by hand, round by round, the sense of it I never had
      The reason for a story of a dam in any culture

A house does not make a person happy
But a house can be a quiet place
With wood smoke and side porch and raised vegetable bed
Where there is the effort made to be your happy self
Maybe

    am blown   am blown   am blown

am/not a Chinese character w/

  game-playing arms

am lust for the presence   (& the fear part, too, let's not pretend—

    (time to return to Duchamp again & his great glass whims of broken
              whistling even

     am cracked & it's good

time for the clunkier translations!

    what will I do what will I do what will I Do

well, try to be a mother who enjoys it
      for one thing

& hope to see I am not useless in other ways

    maybe raise some chickens for eggs?

In the spring of 2011, I resign my tenured position in Chicago,
we sell our apartment in Evanston,
and we buy an 1854 farmhouse in Belfast, Maine and move back.
I take care of my two-year-old son,
join a meditation sangha and a women's group
and teach poetry out of our home.

Claim Song Moon, Abundance Moon, Cutting Moon

you grew some lettuce greens from seedlings
and ate them with lunch
        oh, no   here it is the first of its kind   the poem with seedlings in it

about how you went gladly down into the grain
and came up through a magic tunnel
like Andrea and her neighbor with their clippers on either side of the hedge
calling *helloooo! you sound so close!*
and chopping through to the other voice
and then let the two gardens grow together

you can go into a tunnel ecstatically, even death's
you think so
you believe it's a choice though Linda says no
       (because of the not-self)
but in either case you don't have to use the word "sacrifice"

the moontide is for finding out how to dance in your side yard
       (blindfolded)   (in a hula hoop wrapped with metallic tape) and listening at birds

you are starting to be neighborly

a shiny green hoop at a full time

bits of straw-dead-dry grass in the lawn
despite what your mother-in-law says you don't water
       rain will come at some point (and does)

and here it comes now, so shyly, with lightning
you could feel it earlier on the cool salt-wet breeze
and the mosquitoes at dusk
      (this is the noticing dance)

you don't want to sit still as much this cycle
your bleeding is wavering
      late two days, early four days
not coming on the new moon pierced by stars you see off the porch
at four am to let out the dog who was puking and didn't want to be still either

you are trying to learn to turn around quickly
in your green circle with sparkles
how to keep to your briar like a rabbit and not put yourself out there
        (how?)
how to be blind to the goal or its notion
        (how?)

the truth is you have not yet listened to a tree
you have put your hands in the dirt
but you don't know yet what kind of soft brown bird that was with white-tipped wings
you sometimes forget you live by the ocean
and then you see the ocean and it stops you
with its still and wild utterance
at fair time, bread time
up a hill sunwise to pick the low-bush berry
to love the fullness of summer as its dips over the wheel
toward its own waning

so at least you are starting to consider the act of listening while outdoors
or picking your head up
or going face-first full frontal into the grain

but it's a long tunnel   let me tell you, self

Thunder Hole

Acadia National Park, Mount Desert Island, Maine

1.

Thunder Hole comes back to me in the dream in the form of a dangerous rainstorm that churns up the ocean so that sometimes the waves break over the cement guard wall in front of the town and our newly bought home with the glass walls to face the view. Our home is just behind the guard wall, right on the edge, and we watch the waves crash against our windows, seeming every time to threaten to destroy our home. We could lose everything we have just recently acquired. And we just stand there watching for it, but it doesn't happen.

Elsewhere in the dream, wildly hungry for sex with my own husband, delicious and available and laid out before me like a fine supper. So hungry for him it wakes me up.

This year has brought many dreams of danger coming in from the ocean. And isn't water in a dream for sex?

2.

At the sangha this morning, I sit on a squishy pink cushion and sneeze and sneeze in the new autumn everything, notice how I cannot control my sneeze, but how I can notice how it gathers and goes, gathers and goes. I feel happy and my sneezes are funny to me. Notice: *happy*. Behind me, Margaret's stomach rumbles like someone slurping coffee and I worry about her elderly bird body. Does she eat? Has she ever been someone who has eaten? Notice: *worrying*. Next to her sits Walt, who is contentedly humming either because he is receiving a continual stream of gentle enlightenments during his sitting or because he has fallen asleep. Walt's sleep noise is exactly the noise my husband makes when I go down on him. In this way, we are all connected. And hunger. And sex. And water. Notice.

After seated meditation and walking meditation, there is tea and coffee and talking. We are reading a book with a chapter about how everything is burning, including the burning. I say I am wondering what the place for happiness is if we are supposed to be non-attached. Can we be passionate if we are attaining a serene neutrality? Is contentment still a grasping (at what it is that makes us content), or is it not grasping (because contentment is the state of non-grasping)?

Walt, who is wearing a boatbuilding hat and a boatbuilding t-shirt, says, "When I went to Vietnam, I was just a kid. We went to a village that was burning—actual burning. Some people were carrying their children and running and crying. And some people—I looked right in their eyes and I saw that they had peace with what was. And I wanted that."

I notice that Walt does not say, "I burned the village."

I say, "Isn't this what we do, humans on earth, warring cultures: we see something peaceful and we set it on fire? Because we are terrified of peace?" The sangha does not answer me and I worry that I've made a faux-pas by talking about inherently violent human nature in the space of the sangha. *Worrying.*

Later Walt says, "I have lived for the ocean since I was twelve years old. Now I live on a cliff and I see it every day and every day it is different. I watch the pelican or the waves, and sometimes for a second the separation between me and the ocean is gone and we're one. And then it changes again."

Counting Breaths

1. the path has pine needles softly &
   separation is the problem

2. pull the rock out from under you
   reality is already perfect as it is

1. every knowing of yourself is a fumblehorse situation
   I mean, the problem is enforcing a notion of separateness

2. so I moved to a rural place
   and had a sexy dream of hanging out with a beautiful young man friend
   when the alien mothership started descending
   and we couldn't believe it
   it was just like a movie or a poem

3. it is actually just like the new Lars Van Trier movie
   but I had this dream before I knew about that movie

4. bragging again

1. which is the unbelievable belief?
   that each of us has an inner spirit of boundless love &
   egolessness and can be free of anxiety
   or that someone was born of God and walked on water?

2. enlightenment has nothing to do with being exalted

3.

1. even in the country I dream in celebrity and libido

2. honesty is the sole requirement
   remember: don't try to know anything

1. what's your original face
   teaching without teaching—
   find the original face of the poem

2. the night before I dreamt I'm talking to a guy named Kevin
   about the wonder of the authentic self &

joining hands with nature which speaks its own language
so I have to listen differently
but now Kevin has to go pick up his wife from the airport
Kevin's a Druid, sincerely

1. tree has no ego
   the ego has no sense of humor
   could I turn the light of humor on and erase the shadow of ego?

2. it is a great tragedy to die without knowing who we are

3. dinner at Kal and Linda's 6:30 on Friday

Going Up the Country

We "dropped out,"
but yellow lights outside the bedroom window again tonight.
Cops or the snowplows.

The oil furnace beneath us,
churning like an egg.
We keep it quite cold,
but the winter air is colder still.
A sense of the pioneer about things.

I.e., a wild place for being free
and in love in the country.
Small criminal acts and roadkill.

>   In the parking lot of Reny's,
>   two white-haired women, serious Buddhists
>   buying discount trash bags,
>   stop to talk to me about the poems I read
>   at the American Legion the month before.
>
>   A letter arrives for our daughter
>   addressed to just her name and the street's,
>   no house number.
>   In these ways we are already known.

There are places about which you say
"I'm going up," like a pilgrimage, an ascending.

Written One Year Ago Today, in the Same Mood

White men saying hello to me
hello hello
because I am dripping clear cream   days on end
& they sniff it out, "vibe its vibe"
if it were not for my little copper filament
they'd receptacle me with all their progeny

hold hands, sisters

I'm a curtsier, a skipper, a white girl
but it's Sonia Sanchez I want to get my answers from:

love yourself

be in your body

regardless

yes, I chose to have these children
yes, I love the boy-child dearly,
clearly

but I want to hold hands with my sisters
outside where the seasons dwell

I've been dreaming the dream of the dog I love
but must give away, biting dog,
in order to move ahead

      Take it to the streets & strategize

(the tarot cards said, & scheme)

I dream the dream of the wedding,
the actress, the tents in the backyard
& another woman's husband
& my creaming attraction

but want to hold hands with my sisters
above the clamor of the fucking jealousies

I had a vision of the square hole,
the Jesus-talker on the El platform says,
real as a can of beans
& then silently waits for his train

                                          put it in
                                        put it all in

nothing can snuff out the force field
of my sexual laser beams!
no copper lightbulb!

You are intense, the man said,
& I laughed

asked Meg Reilly to read some wild dreamy roaming hippie poems with me,
with vaginas in them,
& we could switch hair

Go to where your happiness is, Meg said
after telling me about the 19th c. erotic Japanese prints
she found at the Winter Antiques show,
after telling me about getting married & moving to London
& finding a Japanese print for 20 dollars
but worth a thousand

& Nick Demske wrote to say he thinks
maybe he has been a well-trained rapist
for years & is not sure how to continue
but is trying to write poems about it

& last night I dreamed of a red-haired twin brother
met in a canvas tent before a wedding and it was about Evan Lavender Smith

I am naming all these poets
because they are important to my heart
& I like the hair on their heads

I'm off to find my freedom, my unknown

I'm not "staying home" with the baby,
        me & him are going to roam,
        roam freely
        pick up stones we like
        & put them down again
        look at the ocean
        be in our bodies
        bake bread
        bake bread

The days will be all different lengths
& one day I won't drip with this baby power anymore
& I'll have another power
with fur and creases and tinctures in amber dropper bottles

& won't I like to know me then

At Forty

What to do with all this health?
This changing sameness?

An upside-down man in a brown suit, the hermit, the priestess.
Singing "You Are My Sunshine" to the moon group.

Sitting on the sofa with bodies breaking in waves.
Everything keeps coming and I keep saying *yes*.

ACKNOWLEDGMENTS

I am enormously grateful for the community of Belfast, Maine, and surrounding Waldo County. These poems were written because I've been fortunate enough to know you and live among you.

I'm so fortunate to have had Fox Henry Frazier and the team at Agape Editions with me every step of the way on this book. Our editorial process involved cocktail recipes, magic spells, delays due to the births and care-taking of many children, intense conversations about race and other political issues and other deeply human (and often gendered) experiences. This book is so much stronger due to its home at this spiritually-minded, inclusivity-dedicated feminist press.

My thanks to the journals that first published these poems, sometimes in a different form:

American Poetry Review, BathHouse, Conjunctions (online), *Court Green, Crazyhorse, Cura, Elsewhere Magazine, Interim, Kenyon Review, Little Star, Midway Journal, Oakland Review, On and On Screen, Plume, Poetry Northwest, So to Speak, Spoon River Poetry Review, West Branch* and *Women's Studies Quarterly.*

The poem "ORD" was published as "This Is to Find Out about Something" in the anthology *Brute Neighbors: Urban Nature Poetry, Prose and Photography*, edited by Chris Green and Liam Heneghan and published by the DePaul Humanities Center in 2011, and under its current title in *The Rose Metal Press Field Guide to Prose Poetry: Contemporary Poets in Discussion and Practice*, edited by Gary McDowell and F. Daniel Rzicznek (Rose Metal Press, 2010).

The title of this book comes from the song "Little Green Fountain," by Johnny Cash and June Carter Cash.

ABOUT THE AUTHOR

Arielle Greenberg's previous collections of poetry are *I Live in the Country & Other Dirty Poems, Slice, My Kafka Century* and *Given*. She's also the writer of the creative nonfiction book *Locally Made Panties*, the transgenre chapbooks *Shake Her* and *Fa(r)ther Down* and co-author, with Rachel Zucker, of *Home/Birth: A Poemic*. She has co-edited three anthologies, including *Gurlesque*, forthcoming in an expanded digital edition co-edited with Becca Klaver. Arielle's poems and essays have been featured in *Best American Poetry, Labor Day: True Birth Stories by Today's Best Women Writers* and *The Racial Imaginary*, among other anthologies. She wrote a semi-regular column on contemporary poetics for the *American Poetry Review*, and edited a series of essays called *(K)ink: Writing While Deviant* for *The Rumpus*. A former tenured professor in poetry at Columbia College Chicago, she now lives in Belfast, Maine, where she works as a writer and editor and teaches in the community and elsewhere.

www.ingramcontent.com/pod-product-compliance
Lightning Source LLC
Chambersburg PA
CBHW050330120526
44592CB00014B/2127